Wine Journal

*W*ine tasting, like art and music, can be enjoyed by everyone.

A glass of wine has the power to create individual pleasure and, when

shared, has the ability to create lasting friendships. This journal will

help you record those pleasurable experiences and share them with

family and friends. Read about red and white grapes at the beginning

of this journal. Then use the following pages to record your thoughts

on wines you enjoy. Attach a label if you wish...it will help you

remember what to buy.

Happy Tasting!

Red wine is made from red, blue, or purple grapes. The grape juice

is fermented with the skins of the grapes. The skin will give the wine

its color. The skin also has tannin, which is part of the stronger taste

of most red wines. Popular red grapes include Cabernet Sauvignon,

Merlot, Pinot Noir, Shiraz, Zinfandel, Sangiovese, Grenache, and

Cabernet Franc.

Cabernet Sauvignon *(cab-air-nay soov-en-yawn)*

Cabernet Sauvignon is the most famous of the red grapes. At its best, it can produce wines of amazing complexity and structure that can mature and improve with age. Adding to it's allure and credibility is the fact that many of the most distinguished, expensive, and collectible red table wines are made entirely or partly from Cabernet Sauvignon. Because it can be a bit tight and closed in its youth, it is often blended with other grapes. With Merlot, it can soften its edges, add fruitiness, and increase its complexity.

Merlot *(mer-loh)*

Merlot enjoys an excellent reputation for quality. The Merlot grape is a close cousin to Cabernet Sauvignon in many respects. It is lower in tannins and makes wines that mature faster and are softer in texture. Merlot is often blended with Cabernet Sauvignon in order to soften the blend. Merlot is able to mature in regions that are cooler than those required for Cabernet Sauvignon. Merlot varies widely in quality around the world depending on location and producer. Merlot usually has ripe berry components in the bouquet. Its wines tend to be soft, fruity and smooth in texture. Select Merlots can have long aging potential but most are ready to consume in 4 to 8 years.

Pinot Noir (pee-noh nwahr)

Pinot Noir is referred to as the "heartbreak grape" because it is difficult to grow. It is also one of the very best when it is done properly. It has very specific requirements for its growing conditions. It needs warm days and cool nights. If Pinot Noir receives too little heat in the growing season, its wines are thin and pale. If the growing season is too warm, the wines have an overripe, cooked flavor. Pinot Noir can produce wines of stunning complexity. Wines from Pinot Noir are often lighter in color and body. They have much thinner skins than a Merlot. Because of its "lightness" it can be blended with the sparkling wines and adds body, aroma, and richness.

Shiraz (shee-rahz)

Shiraz is becoming one of the most popular wines with consumers and critics. It is a rugged red grape that is grown in a variety of climates. The beauty of Shiraz is that it can flourish in a range of climates. Shiraz came into focus in the cooler climates of the world. The cooler regions of Central Victoria, Coonawarra and Padthaway became known for structured wines that had black cherry, pepper and spice characteristics rather than the chocolate and stewed plums found in warmer climates. Shiraz is known for its fruitiness and spice flavor.

Zinfandel *(zin-fun-DELL)*

Zinfandel is a grape variety that has been important almost exclusively in California. The Zinfandel grape can make solid red wines with good fruit and structure. It was a popular variety with home winemakers during the American prohibition era because its thick skins allowed the grapes to ship without damage. White Zinfandel is a Zinfandel rose that is left slightly sweet with an acid balance. Recent DNA tests indicate that Zinfandel is actually the same as the Primitivo grape found in Italy.

Sangiovese *(sahn-ioe-VAY-zeh)*

This is the workhorse red grape of Italy. It excels in the region of Tuscany, where it's the main ingredient of Chianti and other wines. The hot, dry climate that Tuscany provides is where Sangiovese thrives. Because these climatic criteria generally enhance quantity, rather than quality, it takes careful cultivation and winemaking techniques to produce really excellent wine from this grape. The flavor profile of Sangiovese is fruity, with moderate to high natural acidity and generally a medium-body ranging from firm and elegant to assertive and robust and a finish that can tend towards bitterness. The aroma is generally not as assertive and easily identifiable as Cabernet Sauvignon, for example, but can have a strawberry, blueberry, faintly floral, violet or a plum character.

Grenache (gray-NASH)

The Grenache grape variety is a sweet grape and is one of the most planted in the world. It produces wines that are fruity, full in flavor, and have overtones of spice. Wines made from the Grenache are usually light in color and are often made of blends with other grape-varieties. Grenache resists heat and tolerates limited rainfall. In France it is used in making red and rose (Tavel and Lirac) wines in the Rhone river valley where it is widely planted. Grenache is widely planted in Spain where it is known as Garnacha Tinta. In the United States it is grown in California where it is almost exclusively a blending grape for rose wines.

Cabernet Franc (cab-air-nay FrahN)

Cabernet Franc is grown mainly in the Bordeaux region. In Pomerol and Saint-Emilion it is known as "Bouchet". This grape-variety is also present in the Madiran vines as "Bouchy". Further north, in the Loire Valley and, particularly in Touraine and in Saumur it sometimes appears as "Breton". This is one of the most important red grapes in France, especially in the Loire Valley. Cabernet Franc is a grape-variety which gives small bunches of tiny blackberries. Vine growers appreciate it because it is not demanding and any soil is convenient. Cabernet Franc has a bright and shiny color. It brings strawberry and blackberry aromas. However, because it is less perfumed and structured, it is often associated to other vine-varieties.

White wine's aroma and flavor comes in many different forms. Very rarely does a wine smell or taste of grapes. Nevertheless, the grape variety employed is the single most important determinate of color, aroma, and taste characteristics of the final wine. The six classic white grapes are Chardonnay, Sauvignon Blanc, Riesling, Semillon, Viognier, and Chenin Blanc.

Chardonnay *(shar-don-ay)*

The Chardonnay grape variety is a classic white wine grape grown all around the world. The original fame of Chardonnay comes from its success in the Burgundy and Champagne regions of France. White Burgundy must be made from the Chardonnay grape unless the label indicates it was made from a much less well-known grape, Aligoté. Chardonnay takes oak well, and many higher priced Chardonnays are typically fermented and/or aged in oak barrels. When Chardonnay is aged in oak barrels, it may pick up vanilla overtones in its aromas and flavor. Chardonnay also ages well in the bottle, though it will not age as long as many red wines. It likes slightly cooler climates (warm days/cool nights) and develops less acidity than Sauvignon Blanc. Some producers put their Chardonnay (or some of it) through malolactic fermentation which reduces crispness and brings out a rich, buttery taste. This usually shortens the life of the wine, as far as aging is concerned.

Sauvignon Blanc *(so-vin-yon blonk)*

The Sauvignon Blanc grape is of French origin and is grown extensively in the Bordeaux region where it is blended with Semillon and the upper Loire Valley where it is made as a varietal wine. New Zealand produces some excellent Sauvignon Blancs. Wines labeled fume Blanc are Sauvignon Blanc wines that have seen some oak contact to impart smoky flavors. Sauvignon Blancs will display smoky qualities without any oak treatment. Sauvignon Blancs require a strong acid finish and are best grown in cool to cold climates. Some Australian Sauvignon Blanc, grown in warmer areas, tends to be flat and lack fruit qualities. Often the appearance is near-colorless with colors of light straw to light yellow. Young wines may have a green tinge and aged wines can present deep yellow and golden color. Sauvignon Blanc can present a huge range of flavors from sour green fruits of apples, pears and gooseberries to exotic tropical fruits of melon, mango and blackcurrant.

Riesling *(rees-ling)*

The Riesling is considered one of the 'noble' grape varieties for wine making. It can produce wines of high acidity and elegance in very cool growing conditions. Its wines usually show fresh fruit flavors and a zesty character. Riesling has the ability to produce wines that run the gamut from bone dry to very sweet, but are usually made in dry semi-dry styles. It has perfumey aromas with peach and honeysuckle notes and can develop a 'petrol' nose as it ages. Riesling does best in cool climates and is very resistant to frost. It is planted very widely in the northern European growing regions, and is less popular in other areas of the world.

Semillon (sem-ee-yon)

Semillon has been seen as somewhat dimensionless to most parts of the world and is usually blended. In Australia it is made as a varietal dry white table wine with fabulous success producing fine wines with ageing potential. The Hunter Valley, where it was incorrectly called Riesling for many years, produces some of our country's best Semillons. These wines are rarely oaked and display the distinctive notes of toast and honey with age. Lemon, limes and honey are common in dry styles. Semillon will display wood character of toast without being oaked and as they age this toasty character will grow. Some will show a mineral or steely character with tight acid structure. Botrytis-affected fruits will produce exotic luscious wines of ripe peach, apricot and honey. With barrel aging, flavors of vanilla, caramel, spicy bacon, coconut, cedar and spice will be apparent.

Viognier (vee-ohn-yay)

The Viognier grape was once a little used variety best known in Condrieu, in the northern Rhone Valley of southwestern France. It is experiencing resurgence in popularity as more of it is being planted in California and elsewhere in the world. It makes fruity wines of medium body. Stone fruit aromas (peach and apricot) are often found in wines made from Viognier along with a bit of spice. Depending on the producer's style, the wine matches well with 'Asian Infusion' dishes as well as many foods that are often served with Chardonnay.

Chenin Blanc *(shay-naN blonk)*

Chenin Blanc is a white grape that is commonly grown in the Loire Valley of France, South Africa, and California. It makes white wines that are fragrant and high in acid. Chenin Blanc can make wines that range in style from dry to very sweet depending on decisions made by the winemaker. Because of the high acidity in wines made from Chenin Blanc, they tend to age very well. In Saumur, Chenin Blanc is used to make sparkling wines of notable quality. Chenin Blanc is known elsewhere as Pineau de la Loire. It is the most plated grape in South Africa where its local name is Steen. Chenin Blanc is a high volume producer, so the wines it produces tend to be fairly inexpensive.

Date Purchased 12/1/13   Price   Dated Tasted

Occasion

Winery (Name/Location) *Chateau St. Croix*

Special Designation (Reserve, Bottling)

Region

Vintage

Grape or Blend

Color

Taste

Aroma

Served With

Thoughts/Wine Label

Sunday drive to St. Croix Falls, Wisconsin

Date Purchased   Price   Dated Tasted

Occasion

Winery (Name/Location)

Special Designation (Reserve, Bottling)

Region

Vintage

Grape or Blend

Color

Taste

Aroma

Served With

Thoughts/Wine Label

Date Purchased   Price   Dated Tasted

Occasion

Winery (Name/Location)

Special Designation (Reserve, Bottling)

Region

Vintage

Grape or Blend

Color

Taste

Aroma

Served With

Thoughts/Wine Label

Date Purchased   Price   Dated Tasted

Occasion

Winery (Name/Location)

Special Designation (Reserve, Bottling)

Region

Vintage

Grape or Blend

Color

Taste

Aroma

Served With

Thoughts/Wine Label

Date Purchased   Price   Dated Tasted

Occasion

Winery (Name/Location)

Special Designation (Reserve, Bottling)

Region

Vintage

Grape or Blend

Color

Taste

Aroma

Served With

Thoughts/Wine Label

Date Purchased	Price	Dated Tasted

Occasion

Winery (Name/Location)

Special Designation (Reserve, Bottling)

Region

Vintage

Grape or Blend

Color

Taste

Aroma

Served With

Thoughts/Wine Label

Date Purchased   Price   Dated Tasted

Occasion

Winery (Name/Location)

Special Designation (Reserve, Bottling)

Region

Vintage

Grape or Blend

Color

Taste

Aroma

Served With

Thoughts/Wine Label

Date Purchased   Price   Dated Tasted

Occasion

Winery (Name/Location)

Special Designation (Reserve, Bottling)

Region

Vintage

Grape or Blend

Color

Taste

Aroma

Served With

Thoughts/Wine Label

Date Purchased   Price   Dated Tasted

Occasion

Winery (Name/Location)

Special Designation (Reserve, Bottling)

Region

Vintage

Grape or Blend

Color

Taste

Aroma

Served With

Thoughts/Wine Label

Date Purchased	Price	Dated Tasted

Occasion

Winery (Name/Location)

Special Designation (Reserve, Bottling)

Region

Vintage

Grape or Blend

Color

Taste

Aroma

Served With

Thoughts/Wine Label

Date Purchased   Price   Dated Tasted

Occasion

Winery (Name/Location)

Special Designation (Reserve, Bottling)

Region

Vintage

Grape or Blend

Color

Taste

Aroma

Served With

Thoughts/Wine Label

Date Purchased   Price   Dated Tasted

Occasion

Winery (Name/Location)

Special Designation (Reserve, Bottling)

Region

Vintage

Grape or Blend

Color

Taste

Aroma

Served With

Thoughts/Wine Label

Date Purchased   Price   Dated Tasted

Occasion

Winery (Name/Location)

Special Designation (Reserve, Bottling)

Region

Vintage

Grape or Blend

Color

Taste

Aroma

Served With

Thoughts/Wine Label

Date Purchased	Price	Dated Tasted

Occasion

Winery (Name/Location)

Special Designation (Reserve, Bottling)

Region

Vintage

Grape or Blend

Color

Taste

Aroma

Served With

Thoughts/Wine Label

Date Purchased   Price   Dated Tasted

Occasion

Winery (Name/Location)

Special Designation (Reserve, Bottling)

Region

Vintage

Grape or Blend

Color

Taste

Aroma

Served With

Thoughts/Wine Label

Date Purchased   Price   Dated Tasted

Occasion

Winery (Name/Location)

Special Designation (Reserve, Bottling)

Region

Vintage

Grape or Blend

Color

Taste

Aroma

Served With

Thoughts/Wine Label

Date Purchased   Price   Dated Tasted

Occasion

Winery (Name/Location)

Special Designation (Reserve, Bottling)

Region

Vintage

Grape or Blend

Color

Taste

Aroma

Served With

Thoughts/Wine Label

Date Purchased   Price   Dated Tasted

Occasion

Winery (Name/Location)

Special Designation (Reserve, Bottling)

Region

Vintage

Grape or Blend

Color

Taste

Aroma

Served With

Thoughts/Wine Label

Date Purchased   Price   Dated Tasted

Occasion

Winery (Name/Location)

Special Designation (Reserve, Bottling)

Region

Vintage

Grape or Blend

Color

Taste

Aroma

Served With

Thoughts/Wine Label

Date Purchased	Price	Dated Tasted

Occasion

Winery (Name/Location)

Special Designation (Reserve, Bottling)

Region

Vintage

Grape or Blend

Color

Taste

Aroma

Served With

Thoughts/Wine Label

Date Purchased   Price   Dated Tasted

Occasion

Winery (Name/Location)

Special Designation (Reserve, Bottling)

Region

Vintage

Grape or Blend

Color

Taste

Aroma

Served With

Thoughts/Wine Label

Date Purchased   Price   Dated Tasted

Occasion

Winery (Name/Location)

Special Designation (Reserve, Bottling)

Region

Vintage

Grape or Blend

Color

Taste

Aroma

Served With

Thoughts/Wine Label

Date Purchased   Price   Dated Tasted

Occasion

Winery (Name/Location)

Special Designation (Reserve, Bottling)

Region

Vintage

Grape or Blend

Color

Taste

Aroma

Served With

Thoughts/Wine Label

Date Purchased   Price   Dated Tasted

Occasion

Winery (Name/Location)

Special Designation (Reserve, Bottling)

Region

Vintage

Grape or Blend

Color

Taste

Aroma

Served With

Thoughts/Wine Label

Date Purchased   Price   Dated Tasted

Occasion

Winery (Name/Location)

Special Designation (Reserve, Bottling)

Region

Vintage

Grape or Blend

Color

Taste

Aroma

Served With

Thoughts/Wine Label

Date Purchased	Price	Dated Tasted

Occasion

Winery (Name/Location)

Special Designation (Reserve, Bottling)

Region

Vintage

Grape or Blend

Color

Taste

Aroma

Served With

Thoughts/Wine Label

Date Purchased   Price   Dated Tasted

Occasion

Winery (Name/Location)

Special Designation (Reserve, Bottling)

Region

Vintage

Grape or Blend

Color

Taste

Aroma

Served With

Thoughts/Wine Label

Date Purchased   Price   Dated Tasted

Occasion

Winery (Name/Location)

Special Designation (Reserve, Bottling)

Region

Vintage

Grape or Blend

Color

Taste

Aroma

Served With

Thoughts/Wine Label

Date Purchased   Price   Dated Tasted

Occasion

Winery (Name/Location)

Special Designation (Reserve, Bottling)

Region

Vintage

Grape or Blend

Color

Taste

Aroma

Served With

Thoughts/Wine Label

Date Purchased	Price	Dated Tasted

Occasion

Winery (Name/Location)

Special Designation (Reserve, Bottling)

Region

Vintage

Grape or Blend

Color

Taste

Aroma

Served With

Thoughts/Wine Label

Date Purchased   Price   Dated Tasted

Occasion

Winery (Name/Location)

Special Designation (Reserve, Bottling)

Region

Vintage

Grape or Blend

Color

Taste

Aroma

Served With

Thoughts/Wine Label

Date Purchased   Price   Dated Tasted

Occasion

Winery (Name/Location)

Special Designation (Reserve, Bottling)

Region

Vintage

Grape or Blend

Color

Taste

Aroma

Served With

Thoughts/Wine Label

Date Purchased   Price   Dated Tasted

Occasion

Winery (Name/Location)

Special Designation (Reserve, Bottling)

Region

Vintage

Grape or Blend

Color

Taste

Aroma

Served With

Thoughts/Wine Label

Date Purchased	Price	Dated Tasted

Occasion

Winery (Name/Location)

Special Designation (Reserve, Bottling)

Region

Vintage

Grape or Blend

Color

Taste

Aroma

Served With

Thoughts/Wine Label

Date Purchased	Price	Dated Tasted

Occasion

Winery (Name/Location)

Special Designation (Reserve, Bottling)

Region

Vintage

Grape or Blend

Color

Taste

Aroma

Served With

Thoughts/Wine Label

Date Purchased	Price	Dated Tasted

Occasion

Winery (Name/Location)

Special Designation (Reserve, Bottling)

Region

Vintage

Grape or Blend

Color

Taste

Aroma

Served With

Thoughts/Wine Label

Date Purchased   Price   Dated Tasted

Occasion

Winery (Name/Location)

Special Designation (Reserve, Bottling)

Region

Vintage

Grape or Blend

Color

Taste

Aroma

Served With

Thoughts/Wine Label

Date Purchased	Price	Dated Tasted

Occasion

Winery (Name/Location)

Special Designation (Reserve, Bottling)

Region

Vintage

Grape or Blend

Color

Taste

Aroma

Served With

Thoughts/Wine Label

Date Purchased   Price   Dated Tasted

Occasion

Winery (Name/Location)

Special Designation (Reserve, Bottling)

Region

Vintage

Grape or Blend

Color

Taste

Aroma

Served With

Thoughts/Wine Label

Date Purchased   Price   Dated Tasted

Occasion

Winery (Name/Location)

Special Designation (Reserve, Bottling)

Region

Vintage

Grape or Blend

Color

Taste

Aroma

Served With

Thoughts/Wine Label

Date Purchased   Price   Dated Tasted

Occasion

Winery (Name/Location)

Special Designation (Reserve, Bottling)

Region

Vintage

Grape or Blend

Color

Taste

Aroma

Served With

Thoughts/Wine Label

Date Purchased   Price   Dated Tasted

Occasion

Winery (Name/Location)

Special Designation (Reserve, Bottling)

Region

Vintage

Grape or Blend

Color

Taste

Aroma

Served With

Thoughts/Wine Label

Date Purchased   Price   Dated Tasted

Occasion

Winery (Name/Location)

Special Designation (Reserve, Bottling)

Region

Vintage

Grape or Blend

Color

Taste

Aroma

Served With

Thoughts/Wine Label

Date Purchased	Price	Dated Tasted

Occasion

Winery (Name/Location)

Special Designation (Reserve, Bottling)

Region

Vintage

Grape or Blend

Color

Taste

Aroma

Served With

Thoughts/Wine Label

Date Purchased   Price   Dated Tasted

Occasion

Winery (Name/Location)

Special Designation (Reserve, Bottling)

Region

Vintage

Grape or Blend

Color

Taste

Aroma

Served With

Thoughts/Wine Label

Date Purchased   Price   Dated Tasted

Occasion

Winery (Name/Location)

Special Designation (Reserve, Bottling)

Region

Vintage

Grape or Blend

Color

Taste

Aroma

Served With

Thoughts/Wine Label

Date Purchased	Price	Dated Tasted

Occasion

Winery (Name/Location)

Special Designation (Reserve, Bottling)

Region

Vintage

Grape or Blend

Color

Taste

Aroma

Served With

Thoughts/Wine Label

Date Purchased   Price   Dated Tasted

Occasion

Winery (Name/Location)

Special Designation (Reserve, Bottling)

Region

Vintage

Grape or Blend

Color

Taste

Aroma

Served With

Thoughts/Wine Label

Date Purchased   Price   Dated Tasted

Occasion

Winery (Name/Location)

Special Designation (Reserve, Bottling)

Region

Vintage

Grape or Blend

Color

Taste

Aroma

Served With

Thoughts/Wine Label

Date Purchased   Price   Dated Tasted

Occasion

Winery (Name/Location)

Special Designation (Reserve, Bottling)

Region

Vintage

Grape or Blend

Color

Taste

Aroma

Served With

Thoughts/Wine Label

Date Purchased   Price   Dated Tasted

Occasion

Winery (Name/Location)

Special Designation (Reserve, Bottling)

Region

Vintage

Grape or Blend

Color

Taste

Aroma

Served With

Thoughts/Wine Label

Date Purchased   Price   Dated Tasted

Occasion

Winery (Name/Location)

Special Designation (Reserve, Bottling)

Region

Vintage

Grape or Blend

Color

Taste

Aroma

Served With

Thoughts/Wine Label

Date Purchased _____ Price _____ Dated Tasted _____

Occasion _____

Winery (Name/Location) _____

Special Designation (Reserve, Bottling) _____

Region _____

Vintage _____

Grape or Blend _____

Color _____

Taste _____

Aroma _____

Served With _____

Thoughts/Wine Label _____

_____

_____

_____

_____

_____

_____

_____

_____

_____

_____

_____

_____

Date Purchased   Price   Dated Tasted

Occasion

Winery (Name/Location)

Special Designation (Reserve, Bottling)

Region

Vintage

Grape or Blend

Color

Taste

Aroma

Served With

Thoughts/Wine Label

Date Purchased   Price   Dated Tasted

Occasion

Winery (Name/Location)

Special Designation (Reserve, Bottling)

Region

Vintage

Grape or Blend

Color

Taste

Aroma

Served With

Thoughts/Wine Label

Date Purchased   Price   Dated Tasted

Occasion

Winery (Name/Location)

Special Designation (Reserve, Bottling)

Region

Vintage

Grape or Blend

Color

Taste

Aroma

Served With

Thoughts/Wine Label

Date Purchased   Price   Dated Tasted

Occasion

Winery (Name/Location)

Special Designation (Reserve, Bottling)

Region

Vintage

Grape or Blend

Color

Taste

Aroma

Served With

Thoughts/Wine Label

Date Purchased   Price   Dated Tasted

Occasion

Winery (Name/Location)

Special Designation (Reserve, Bottling)

Region

Vintage

Grape or Blend

Color

Taste

Aroma

Served With

Thoughts/Wine Label

Date Purchased   Price   Dated Tasted

Occasion

Winery (Name/Location)

Special Designation (Reserve, Bottling)

Region

Vintage

Grape or Blend

Color

Taste

Aroma

Served With

Thoughts/Wine Label

Date Purchased   Price   Dated Tasted

Occasion

Winery (Name/Location)

Special Designation (Reserve, Bottling)

Region

Vintage

Grape or Blend

Color

Taste

Aroma

Served With

Thoughts/Wine Label

Date Purchased   Price   Dated Tasted

Occasion

Winery (Name/Location)

Special Designation (Reserve, Bottling)

Region

Vintage

Grape or Blend

Color

Taste

Aroma

Served With

Thoughts/Wine Label

Date Purchased   Price   Dated Tasted

Occasion

Winery (Name/Location)

Special Designation (Reserve, Bottling)

Region

Vintage

Grape or Blend

Color

Taste

Aroma

Served With

Thoughts/Wine Label

Date Purchased   Price   Dated Tasted

Occasion

Winery (Name/Location)

Special Designation (Reserve, Bottling)

Region

Vintage

Grape or Blend

Color

Taste

Aroma

Served With

Thoughts/Wine Label

Date Purchased	Price	Dated Tasted

Occasion

Winery (Name/Location)

Special Designation (Reserve, Bottling)

Region

Vintage

Grape or Blend

Color

Taste

Aroma

Served With

Thoughts/Wine Label

Date Purchased   Price   Dated Tasted

Occasion

Winery (Name/Location)

Special Designation (Reserve, Bottling)

Region

Vintage

Grape or Blend

Color

Taste

Aroma

Served With

Thoughts/Wine Label

Date Purchased   Price   Dated Tasted

Occasion

Winery (Name/Location)

Special Designation (Reserve, Bottling)

Region

Vintage

Grape or Blend

Color

Taste

Aroma

Served With

Thoughts/Wine Label

Date Purchased   Price   Dated Tasted

Occasion

Winery (Name/Location)

Special Designation (Reserve, Bottling)

Region

Vintage

Grape or Blend

Color

Taste

Aroma

Served With

Thoughts/Wine Label

Date Purchased   Price   Dated Tasted

Occasion

Winery (Name/Location)

Special Designation (Reserve, Bottling)

Region

Vintage

Grape or Blend

Color

Taste

Aroma

Served With

Thoughts/Wine Label

Date Purchased   Price   Dated Tasted

Occasion

Winery (Name/Location)

Special Designation (Reserve, Bottling)

Region

Vintage

Grape or Blend

Color

Taste

Aroma

Served With

Thoughts/Wine Label